THE HAYES BOOK OF
ACTS OF COURAGE

Written by
Stef Donev, Mary Kaiser Donev,
Teri Kelly and J. Terry Winik

Editors:
Nadia Pelowich
Paul Hayes
Curtis Rush

Illustrated by
Rob Johannsen, Raffi Anderian
J. Terry Winik

Cover by
David Bathurst

Penworthy Publishing Company, 219 North Milwaukee St., Milwaukee, Wisconsin 53202

Copyright 1986 by Hayes Publishing Ltd.
Burlington, Ontario

ISBN 0-87617-022-X

CONTENTS

The London Sparrow

The wanted posters were all over the villages near Yangcheng, in Central China. The Japanese Army was offering a $100.00 reward, a great deal of money in war-torn China in 1940, for the capture of "the small woman, known as Ai Weh Teh."

The Japanese Army wanted her alive. They, themselves, would see to her death - and they would make sure it was slow and painful - but only after she had been questioned.

Ai Weh Teh was a spy for the Nationalist Chinese. At least that's what the invading Japanese Army considered her to be.

But Ai Weh Teh, as the Chinese called her, didn't think of herself as a spy. The small woman, whose Chinese name translated into "The Virtuous One," saw herself only as Gladys Aylward, a British-born former London parlor-maid who had come to China in 1932 as a Christian missionary.

And now, eight years later, "The London Sparrow," as she was also known, was in the middle of a war.

The Japanese had invaded China in 1937. The fighting was fierce, and the Nationalist Chinese Army, under General Chiang Kai-shek, was being pushed back. By the end of that year, all of northeast China was under Japanese control.

The next year, the war reached Yangcheng, Aylward's village. Japanese bombers attacked and Aylward's mission, "The Inn of the Sixth Happiness," was almost completely destroyed. Instead of giving up, Ai Weh Teh cared for the orphans and the wounded - hundreds of them.

For the next two years, she did what she could for the Chinese in her area, helping the sick, the wounded, the refugees and especially the orphans. She also helped the Nationalist Chinese government and troops who were defending the area. This was why the Japanese invaders called her a "spy" and why they would do anything to stop her!

Ai Weh Teh was afraid she would be captured. She also knew what might happen to the orphans and other children who lived at her mission. She had seen what the invaders had done to others — men, women and children — and the terrible sight of their broken bodies would live in her mind forever.

Aylward would have to escape, but she wasn't going alone. She wasn't going to leave her children behind!

In April of 1940, with the Japanese Army pushing closer and closer, Aylward gathered up the 100 children at her mission and prepared them for a journey. She was determined to lead her charges away from the battle zone, over the mountains and across the Hwang Ho, the famous Yellow River, to where safety awaited in Siam.

Aylward and her children spent a month traveling through war torn China. Hiding from Japanese patrols, they lived in constant fear. Food was scarce, but their weak and undernourished bodies pushed on, stopping to rest only when Aylward felt it was safe.

Finally, they reached the Hwang Ho. On the other side lay safety. The Chinese, however, had moved all the ferries to the far side of the river to delay the Japanese Army's approach. How would "The London Sparrow" get across?

For three days Aylward and her small charges waited, praying for a miracle. As they prayed the Japanese were getting closer and closer.

Finally, their miracle happened. A Nationalist Chinese officer appeared. Aylward explained their need to cross the river and the officer agreed to arrange boats for them.

At last they touched the shore of the other side. Although their journey wasn't over, the road ahead would be easier.

In time, Aylward and her children reached Siam. Before she could rest, she made certain her children would be taken care of. Then, with her task accomplished, she collapsed, giving in to the typhus and pneumonia that had tormented her for so long.

With the help of the American Red Cross and other missionaries in Siam, Aylward again found her strength.

"The Virtuous One" continued to open and run other orphanages until her death in 1970, in Taiwan.

ONE MAN'S DREAM

The Rev. Martin Luther King, Jr. had a dream. "I have a dream that one day this nation will rise up and live out the true meaning of its creed: we hold these truths to be self-evident that all men are created equal."

The black Alabama minister, who won the Nobel Peace Prize in 1964, took his dream of racial equality from the slums of the nation to the White House. "I have a dream that my four little children will one day live in a nation where they will not be judged by the color of their skin but by the content of their character. I have a dream that one day in the red hills of Georgia sons of former slaves and sons of former slave owners will be able to sit down together at the table of brotherhood."

Throughout the sixties, Martin Luther King led, or was involved in, countless "sit-ins" and marches from Alabama to Washington, D.C. Time after time he was threatened, attacked and arrested, but nothing could stop this leader of men. He would not let his voice be silenced. Beaten, he would resurface to help lead the struggle, the nonviolent fight for equal rights.

Martin Luther King was assassinated on April 4, 1968. His great voice had been silenced, but his dream lives on in the hearts of men, and he is credited with being one of the strongest powers in getting the Bill of Rights passed by both the U.S. Congress and Senate, revitalizing the American dream of equality, fairness and justice for all — a dream all mankind can share.

A SEARCH FOR A CURE

It was called the "red death," and it terrified all Europe. There was hope for ending the killer disease known as smallpox. But it meant placing an eight-year-old boy's life on the line. Jamie Phipps didn't know that.

The English child only knew that both his father and mother looked worried. And that made him a little worried also.

When Jamie's parents agreed to let their son be vaccinated against the dreaded disease, the Phipps family had no guarantee the boy would live. Mrs. Phipps had lost both her mother and sister to smallpox, but Jamie was a healthy young boy! They had a choice: either they could say "no" and risk the possibility that Jamie would get the disease, or they could agree to the vaccination, which might increase his chances against the disease. It might even make him immune to it.

Their decision lay in their faith of Dr. Edward Jenner. For twenty-six years, Dr. Jenner had searched for a smallpox cure. Now, he was certain he'd found the answer, but no one yet had tried his proposed remedy. If Jamie tried it — if he were vaccinated — all Europe would see, and they might be saved just as easily!

It was May 14, 1796, when Jamie rolled up his sleeve for Dr. Jenner. His parents smiled encouragingly as their son's arm was inoculated with cowpox, a common infection milkers caught from their cows. For years, Dr. Jenner had observed people with cowpox, and he'd noticed they were among the few who never got the terrible disease of smallpox. There was a link, he knew. He would not have allowed Jamie to be inoculated if he knew the boy would be harmed.

Inoculated with a dose of smallpox, Jamie would become mildly sick for a few days, that was all. When his sickness was over, he should be safe forever from catching the dreaded disease. Smallpox could kill or leave its victims blind or insane. If cowpox worked against it, a major breakthrough awaited.

After Jamie was inoculated came the period of waiting. On the seventh day, Jamie felt an aching in his armpits, and two days later, he suffered chills. Shivering in his bed, he complained of a headache, and when food was brought in, he turned his face away. A rash developed and a fever came on. That night was a restless one as Jamie tossed and turned. Dr. Jenner assured the boy's parents that Jamie's rash was not the familiar sign of "red death." Cowpox produced a similar rash. Dr. Jenner wrote to a close friend: "I was astonished at the close resemblance of the pustules in some of their stages. . . . But now listen to the most delightful part of my story. The boy has since been inoculated for the smallpox, which, as I ventured to predict, produced no effect."

That tenth day, Jamie awoke feeling perfectly well. As he grew older, he kept close ties with Dr. Jenner and was vaccinated for smallpox some twenty times throughout his life. Jamie was walking proof of Dr. Jenner's cure. Yet many were not convinced. Though Jamie Phipps lived to a ripe old age, others, who refused the cowpox inoculation, died of the "red death." Those who survived it were left deeply scarred by the smallpox rash.

Nearly one hundred and fifty years would pass before Europe and North America were rid of the disease. In many of the poor countries around the world, smallpox remained an epidemic, and as long as the disease flourished somewhere, it was still a constant threat. If someone infected with smallpox traveled to a smallpox-free area, the disease could spread.

In 1966, an organization called WHO — World Health Organization — began a mission to wipe out smallpox once and for all. It wanted to reach its goal in ten years. This disease, which had taken the lives of so many, would be the first disease "killed" by man. But many did not think this was possible. Everyone with the disease would have to be found, as well as those who had come in contact with the infected persons.

In 1977, Ali Maow Maalin, a hospital cook in Somalia, was the last recorded case of smallpox. WHO believed it had the disease beaten.

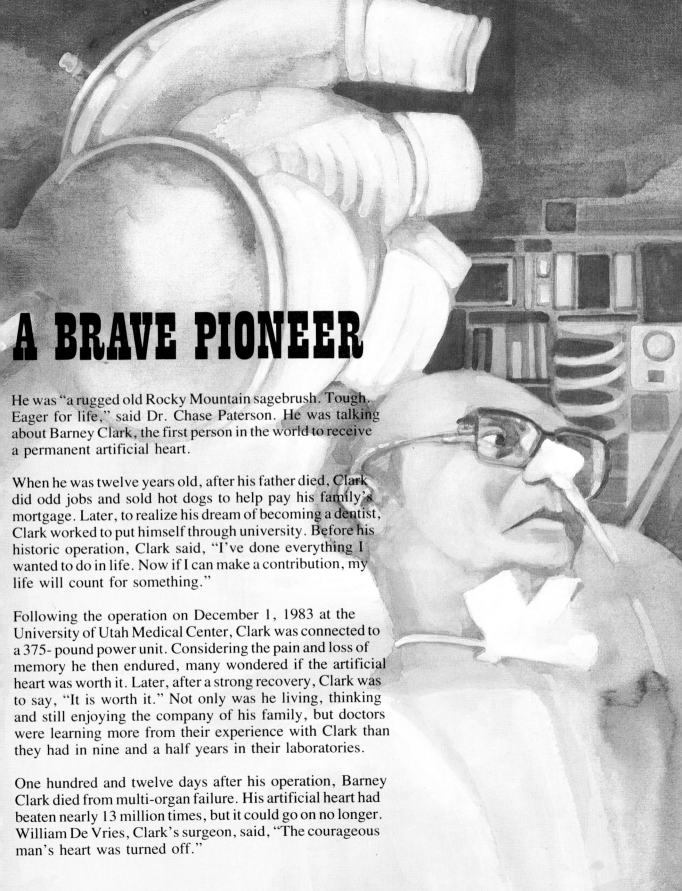

A BRAVE PIONEER

He was "a rugged old Rocky Mountain sagebrush. Tough. Eager for life," said Dr. Chase Paterson. He was talking about Barney Clark, the first person in the world to receive a permanent artificial heart.

When he was twelve years old, after his father died, Clark did odd jobs and sold hot dogs to help pay his family's mortgage. Later, to realize his dream of becoming a dentist, Clark worked to put himself through university. Before his historic operation, Clark said, "I've done everything I wanted to do in life. Now if I can make a contribution, my life will count for something."

Following the operation on December 1, 1983 at the University of Utah Medical Center, Clark was connected to a 375- pound power unit. Considering the pain and loss of memory he then endured, many wondered if the artificial heart was worth it. Later, after a strong recovery, Clark was to say, "It is worth it." Not only was he living, thinking and still enjoying the company of his family, but doctors were learning more from their experience with Clark than they had in nine and a half years in their laboratories.

One hundred and twelve days after his operation, Barney Clark died from multi-organ failure. His artificial heart had beaten nearly 13 million times, but it could go on no longer. William De Vries, Clark's surgeon, said, "The courageous man's heart was turned off."

Mama Narc

The middle-aged motherly looking woman trembled as she got back into her car following a meeting in a private home in Queens, New York. Carefully, she placed the small package on the seat next to her, then turned to her teenaged son, Jorge:

"Son, they just gave me a kilo of cocaine."

In 1983 that 2.2 pound package of Colombian cocaine - an illegal and highly addictive drug - was worth $30,000.

Three months later, she would be given another consignment of Colombian cocaine to sell; only this one would be 24 kilos of 90 percent pure cocaine worth $12 million!

To Mrs. Torres and her family, who had immigrated to the U.S.A. from Central America in 1975, $12 million was an amount too huge even to begin to understand. But she wasn't in it for the money. This 42-year-old mother of four wanted only one thing: to stop the spreading of a drug that had destroyed her eldest son. But how she got the opportunity to do so was by pure chance.

The owner of a jewelry store where she worked was a friend whose kindness she'd learned to trust. Once he had even lent her money for the down payment on her house. So when Mrs. Torres stumbled onto several bags of white powder at the store it took her some time to believe it could really be cocaine.

Mrs. Torres later said that while she truly cared for her friend, she didn't feel she had any choice in the matter.

"I thought if I were to cooperate, some other parents would not suffer how we have suffered with our son."

At first, the police didn't know what to make of her. She was just not the sort of informer they were used to dealing with. What's more, she refused any money. But she did have information on a Colombian connection, information about the same drug traffickers that the police had been trying to catch for a long time. So, Mrs. Torres was entered on the books as "Confidential Informant No. SCT-84-000."

Within a matter of months she would help break the biggest cocaine smuggling ring in U.S. history, closing down a $3.5 billion Colombian operation! Mrs. Torres, pretending to be a buyer, would get the evidence the police needed to break the ring.

For months Mrs. Torres lived in the dangerous world of espionage. She was a double agent leading three different lives: wife and mother, drug dealer, and police undercover agent. She was "wired" with concealed tape recorders to record conversations with drug dealers. She ate and drank with people who would kill her if they even suspected that she was a police spy.

When the dealer gave her drugs to sell on consignment she was supposed to sell the drugs, collect the money and return to the dealers with the cash. Of course, she did not really sell them, but gave them to the police who would then give her money for the dealers. The police kept the drugs as evidence and recorded the serial numbers of the money they gave her. That way, when they arrested the dealers and took the money back, they could prove that the money was obtained from the sale of illegal drugs. But she had to contend with police and government foul-ups. Often the police were late in paying her.

Once, the police had to move her and her family into hiding because she owed the traffickers $12 million for the drugs she had turned over. The drug dealers were looking for her. Her home was torn apart. If she didn't come up with the money, she would be killed.

Finally, the police had all the evidence they needed, and on a series of lightning raids, 11 people were arrested. But through what the police describe as an "administrative error," Eduardo Mera and Severo Escobar - the top two men in the drug ring - were let out on "personal recognizance." They didn't even have to post bail! All they had to do was "promise" that they would show up for trial. They are still missing.

Mrs. Torres received no reward money.

Today, she and her family live somewhere in the U.S.A. under new names supplied by the U.S. Government's witness protection program.

Trevor Ferrell's Gift

Trevor Ferrell was only 11 years old when he first started prowling the late-night streets of Philadelphia - looking for people to help.

He began his personal "mission" after seeing a TV news special about the poor and homeless who lived in the winter streets. He could not believe this sort of thing was happening in Philadelphia which was so widely known as the "City of Brotherly Love." But Trevor did more than just feel sorry for the poor he saw on television. He did something about it.

"I couldn't believe that people lived that way. I knew there were some poor people," said Trevor, "but I thought they were in India, not here."

After the December 1983 television show, Trevor convinced his parents to drive him the 18 miles from their suburban home into the city. He went bearing a treasured gift - a pillow and blanket from his own bed.

The Ferrell family drove around the streets until they found a ragged man huddled on the sidewalk. Trevor asked his parents to stop the car. On this bitter cold night, with his pillow and blanket under his arm, he might have seemed to the man like an angel. Thankful for the gifts, the man gave Trevor a huge smile and said, merely, "God bless you!"

Trevor felt he had "a mission" to these people. Again he came two nights later, bringing one of his mother's old coats. He gave it to a woman who was shivering with the cold. She accepted it gratefully.

Although Trevor's parents were nervous, not knowing what sort of people Trevor might encounter on the street, they drove him back night after night. He brought what clothing his family could spare.

Soon, news of his "mission" spread. Donations of clothing, blankets and money began to pour in. One person even donated a Volkswagen van. With it, Trevor was able to carry sandwiches and hot meals as well as clothing to the street people. Trevor proved that the "City of Brotherly Love" was not just a name without a reason - it was a way of life.

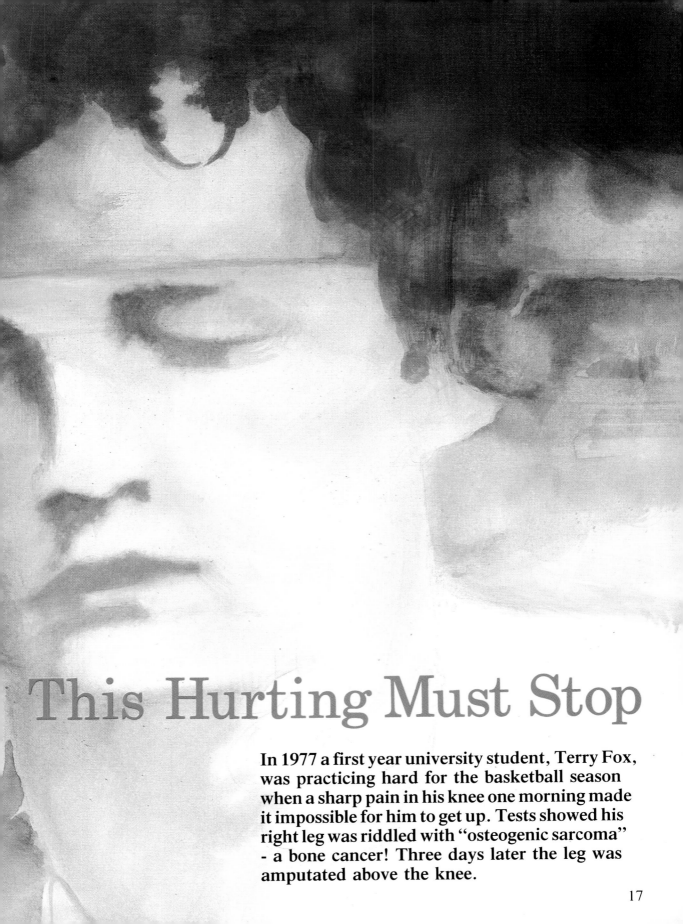

This Hurting Must Stop

In 1977 a first year university student, Terry Fox, was practicing hard for the basketball season when a sharp pain in his knee one morning made it impossible for him to get up. Tests showed his right leg was riddled with "osteogenic sarcoma" - a bone cancer! Three days later the leg was amputated above the knee.

Terry, a young man who had wanted to be a physical education teacher, had to begin the building of new dreams. It was not easy to erase a future he thought was his, and it was even harder to build a new one after being suddenly and severely handicapped, but Terry, raising his chin courageously, did just that.

Inspired by an article on Dick Traum, a one-legged athlete who ran in the New York City Marathon, Terry started thinking, "I can do that." But there would be long, hard months ahead. The courage of other cancer victims gave him strength, and the pain that lined their faces provided the seed for Terry's dream — to end that suffering! One way he could do this, he thought, was to raise money to fight the ravaging disease.

Only three weeks after his leg was amputated, Terry was learning to walk with his artificial leg - or prosthesis. It would be nearly three years before his cross-Canada run would begin but almost immediately he embarked on its preparation, getting himself back into shape for the challenge.

Joining the Vancouver Cablecars team, he learned to play wheelchair basketball, a feat made more difficult because of his urge to jump from his chair. Deeply frustrated, he learned control and endured. Terry was on the team when the Cablecars won the basketball trophy at the National Wheelchair Games in Edmonton.

In February, 1979, roughly two years after his amputation, Terry began training for his run. From half a mile on his first day his daily mileage would increase to fifteen after just nine months! His good leg suffered from the extra pounding, and the artificial leg - designed for walking, not running - caused blisters and bleeding. "It was like running on hot coals," he said.

In spite of the great discomfort that came with each step, nothing would stop him. Each morning he rose with the dawn to train, and in August of that year he entered the Prince George Marathon in Northern British Columbia. Just minutes after the last two-legged runner completed the race, Terry crossed the finish line feeling as though he'd won hands down!

Almost from the beginning, the idea to run across Canada was clear in Terry's mind, but although he'd mentioned it to a close friend, he'd said nothing to his family. As his mother lounged before the television set, Terry entered the room.

"Mom, I'm going to run across Canada."

"You're not," said his mother.

"Yes, I am."

"Terry, you're not!"

But Terry's mind was made up. He composed a letter to Imperial Oil asking for gasoline, another to The Ford Motor Company requesting a vehicle, and yet another to Adidas asking for running shoes and money. All companies replied with a "YES!"

The national office of the Canadian Cancer Society was behind him in promoting the run, though society officials weren't confident of its success. Terry wanted to raise money for cancer. His ultimate dream was to see a dollar donated by every Canadian. Though the Cancer Society officials shared his dream, they did not think Terry's cause would attract much attention. Terry, however, had the greatest confidence in his project, and he'd worked hard to get it going. That kind of optimism deserved support.

Pacific Western Airlines offered transportation to Winnipeg and Labatts Brewery donated beer for a dance organized to raise money for Terry's living expenses as he traveled. War Amputations of Canada would repair and replace Terry's artificial leg whenever necessary, they said, and with that Terry was ready. He had gained weight, his good leg was muscular and stronger than it had ever been, and even before he made his first step toward his cross-country race, Terry had run over 3,000 miles in training. He knew he could do it!

In a symbolic act which marked the beginning of his run from coast to coast, Terry dipped his artificial leg into the Atlantic Ocean. When he reached the Pacific, he said, he would end his journey with the same ceremony.

Terry started in Newfoundland, and it wasn't long before his "run for cancer" became a hot news item. As he passed through the town of Port aux Basques, people crowded the roadside, cheering him on. In this town alone, a total of $10,000 was collected — one dollar from every person who lived there. Terry was thrilled with the success of the fund-raising, but he wished there was more time to meet and talk with the people.

Initially, he had enjoyed meeting Canadians, taking them up on invitations to visit their homes. But as the public grew more aware of him, he had little time to spare. Besides running a full day until his muscles ached, Terry gave talks at schools and spoke to other audiences about what he was doing and why. The Canadian Cancer Society had set up a busy itinerary for Terry, and this, combined with interviews for newspapers and television, took nearly every spare moment he had.

Becoming a popular news item, however, did not necessarily ensure support for his cause. The city streets of Halifax did not greet him as had the small town of Port aux Basques. There were no people lining the sidewalks, but more importantly, there was little money donated. That evening when Terry appeared for a talk he was scheduled to give, the audience numbered just over a handful. Terry was discouraged. Somehow the news of his run had not been properly publicized, or perhaps the people were misunderstanding what he was doing.

"People seem to forget what I'm doing this for," he said to the city's newspaper, The Halifax Mail Star. "They think I am running across Canada on some kind of ego trip. It is a personal challenge, but I'm trying to raise as much money as I can...I need their support."

It was May 21, 1980. Terry's dream of a dollar from every person was a long way off.

More and more, people opened their eyes to what was really happening — and they opened their hearts. Thousands followed his run in the newspapers and on television. By seeing Terry as an individual, as a kid with a great deal of courage, the public was seeing, closer than ever, a victim of cancer. And the more real Terry became, the more real was the threat of cancer. As Terry continued on his run, donations poured in.

He had crossed five provinces in ten weeks, but Ontario seemed endless. As he entered Nathan Phillips Square in Toronto, thousands gathered to cheer his cause at the largest reception he'd yet received. More donations flowed in.

Terry had hoped to reach the west coast by September, but it was late August when he began to feel exhausted and rundown. His energy was fading and he had to rest more frequently. It was with the greatest force of will that he plodded on. Finally, just outside Thunder Bay, fatigue and a blunt pain in his chest forced Terry to stop.

X-rays confirmed that Terry had cancer of the lungs.

He had a dream to see one dollar from every Canadian donated toward cancer research. Before he died, he would realize that dream. Although Terry had been forced to stop the run, Canadians took up where he left off. Terry watched from his hospital room as CTV network gave a tribute to him in a five-hour campaign for donations.

A telegram from Prime Minister Trudeau said, ". . . the whole country is pulling for you."

Each year, as cities and towns across Canada hold the "Terry Fox Run," Canadians continue to fight for Terry's dream.

Hang On

"Hang on, Mom, I'll get through."

Those words became a litany to 19-year-old Doug Rickard. During the week he spent in the frozen woods of Northern Ontario, Doug would repeat them many times. They were the strength behind every plodding step.

As he trudged through knee-high snow, Doug's mind often drifted to the face of his mother. Felled by a stroke she'd lain pale and stricken, her left side paralyzed. If she didn't see a doctor soon, she could die - that was days ago. Doug could hardly remember how many...the hours had merged into one endless trek. But though his feet were numbed with cold, Doug barely stopped. His mother was counting on him. He had to find help!

The young Cree Indian, with his father, mother and two brothers, was trapping in the winter of 1983 up along Hudson Bay. Where they'd made their camp there was no radio, no plane, no Jeep, nor Snowmobile. It was in these remote areas that the animals were most plentiful, but where people were few. The nearest road was almost 50 miles away; 50 miles on a map, but closer to 100 miles considering the rough countryside and snowdrifts.

But as instantly as his mother suffered the stroke, Doug began preparing for his journey. Packing a minimum of supplies — knife, rope, tea, dried beaver meat, a sleeping bag and snowshoes — Doug watched as his father drew the vague lines of a map on a scrap of brown paper. Taking up his .22 rifle, he left with his father's good wishes.

For seven days he fought the harsh northern temperatures, stopping only long enough to catch a few hours' sleep. He would stop to make a fire, and warmed by the flames and the tea he'd made, he'd regain some strength. No sooner had he stopped than he grew impatient to move...his mother could be dying!

Doug studied the map once again. Sometimes he was certain he was cutting the right path and other times he was haunted by the chilling thought that he was lost. It was the seventh day of his journey. Should he not have reached the road before now?

At last, with his energy all but gone, he saw the Smokey Falls Road. Renewed with hope, he ran and stumbled toward it.

It was deserted.

Steeped in silence, it seemed a vehicle had not passed in some time. Would it be much longer before someone drove by? How long could his mother last? How long could he last?

Finally, after hours of following the road, the sound of a vehicle could be heard in the distance. Doug listened to make sure he wasn't imagining it when, around a bend, a truck approached. Doug began waving furiously, and the truck came to a stop. In it were two Ontario Hydro workers.

"My mother's had a stroke," Doug said. They were the first words he had spoken to another human being since he'd left his family seven days before.

The Hydro crew drove to the deserted Kipling dam and called the Ontario Provincial Police. An hour later, a helicopter arrived. An Ontario Provincial Police officer and an ambulance attendant were already on board.

It was only then that they realized how far the young Indian had walked - nearly 100 miles!

It took the helicopter less than an hour to arrive at the camp, covering the same distance that Doug had spent an entire week walking. When they got there his mother was resting.

"I was worried about you, son," she said as she was loaded aboard the helicopter.

The Ontario Provincial Police gave Doug Rickard an O.P.P. Bravery Award. As Constable Louis Cautier put it:

"There's nothing there but bush, yet he crossed that country without a compass or a real map. He thought his mother was going to die, so he just did it. It was an incredible achievement."

RUN

Terry Fox's heroic fight against cancer has inspired millions of men, women and children around the world to raise money for cancer research. Some of these people, like Jeff Keith and Steve Fonyo, are cancer victims themselves.

In 1984, Keith, then 22, finished a 3,200-mile run across the United States, from Boston to Los Angeles. A native of Fairfield, Connecticut, who received the American Cancer Society's Courage Award from U.S. President Ronald Reagan, Keith had lost his right leg to cancer in 1974.

Canadian Steve Fonyo, who lost his left leg to cancer when he was 12, remembers first being inspired by Terry Fox's run, then shattered by his death. In 1984, when he was just 18, he launched his own Journey for Lives, continuing the fight for a cure that Terry Fox had started. Beginning in Newfoundland, Steve ran through a bitter winter, completing his run in Victoria, B.C., in 1985.

EDITH CAVELL

In the dying words of Edith Cavell: "Patriotism is not enough." - she summed up her life.

By the time World War I started in 1914, the English nurse had been heading a teaching hospital in Belgium for seven years. Unlike thousands of others who fled the continent to escape the attacking German armies, Cavell stayed. She had a hospital to run.

Cavell and her nurses worked around the clock, caring for the wounded on both sides of the war. Then, just two months after the fighting broke out, Cavell had to make a decision — one that could bring about her death.

Two wounded men showed up at her hospital. Wearing civilian clothes, they looked like most of the refugees who passed through the area. In fact, they were British soldiers who were hiding out from the Germans, trying to get back home to England. Risking their own lives, the two men told her the truth. Then they asked the key question: "Will you help us?"

Cavell did not hesitate. After taking care of their wounds, she hid them.

But what was to become of the men? They were in the middle of enemy territory! If they were just to walk out the door and try to make it back to England on their own, it could mean their lives! Cavell arranged to have secret couriers guide them to the neutral territory of Holland.

Within a short time, more soldiers were to come. They were guided along the escape route planned by Cavell and members of the Belgian Resistance movement. Eventually, these men could return to fight the enemy. Cavell helped not only British, but French and Belgian soldiers as well.

At one time there were as many as 18 soldiers hidden in the hospital. Cavell's hospital was the most important stop on the "underground" journey to freedom.

She helped anyone who came to her in need and so when George Garton Quien came to her posing as a Paris doctor, she did not think twice about opening the hospital to him. He carried a forged identity card - and he was a spy! He said he had heard about the "underground." Could she help him escape?

Cavell trusted him and allowed him to stay for a few days. He needed rest, he said, before going on to the border. While at the hospital, he discovered the details about the escape route.

When he left, she still had no idea of his true identity but soon afterwards, all of Cavell's friends in the Belgian Resistance were arrested. A few days later, three soldiers, stern-faced and with rifles in hand, showed up at the hospital door. They knew about the escape route, they said, they knew what she'd been up to in hiding prisoners! Now it would all stop! The underground route would be cut - finished! - because they were there to take her away.

Cavell didn't deny that she had helped fugitives on their way to the frontier. She admitted it - proudly!

Forced from the hospital, she was taken prisoner and thrown into an overcrowded jail. Crammed shoulder to shoulder with unwashed and starving bodies, Cavell remained for ten weeks until her trial. When the day finally came to have her "case" judged, Cavell did not expect miracles. What she had done was not something she would deny, not even if it meant her life to lie about it. She was glad for the lives she had helped save, even now. What she had done in planning the underground escape route was something she would do a thousand times over if she had the chance.

But she would not have the chance.

Her trial lasted only five minutes, just long enough for her to admit that she had helped 200 English, French and Belgians to freedom across the border.

The penalty was death.

Shortly before she faced the firing squad on October 12, 1915, she told a chaplain who visited her that: "Standing as I do in view of God and Eternity, I realize that patriotism is not enough. I must have no hatred or bitterness towards anyone."

Cavell's body was returned to England, the land she loved. Crowds lined the streets when her coffin left Westminster Abbey for burial. Inspired by her death, 40,000 men enlisted in the British army.

Angel of the Battlefield

Clara Barton was working as an office patent clerk when the American Civil War broke out. It wasn't long, however, before the small woman set down her pen and papers to investigate the news of suffering which reached her town. Soldiers, she'd heard, who might live if they were tended to, lay dying slowly on the battlefields.

Clara changed this. Responding to the needs of the wounded, she went out every day to the war site where she bandaged the bleeding and fed the hungry. Among the soldiers she became known as the "angel of the battlefield," but her acts of compassion were not to end with the war.

Although peacetime followed, Clara knew suffering continued. Epidemics, disease, starvation and poor living conditions begged attention and so on May 21, 1881, she founded an organization whose purpose was to aid victims of both war and natural disasters. This organization was the American Red Cross.

Even today, more than 100 years later, the American Red Cross continues to aid the needy with outposts and hospitals throughout the world. Through the hands of others like her, Clara's charity continues to reach out to victims.

Galileo's Quest

For centuries, scientists have struggled to decode the riddles of our universe. This unending search for truth has been complicated by superstition, tradition and envy. When genius tackles one of nature's riddles it faces not only a puzzle but also the reluctance of others to accept its solution. Such was the case when Galileo Galilei applied his genius to the scientific problems of his day.

The world into which Galileo Galilei was born in 1564 believed the earth was the center of the universe. It was accepted that the sun, the planets and even the stars moved around the earth while it remained stationary. This belief was called the geocentric theory of the universe. Opposing this theory would be Galileo's lifelong challenge.

Galileo would take up what is called the heliocentric theory. Introduced by Nicholas Copernicus more than 100 years before, this theory stated that the sun was at the center of the solar system and that the earth was merely one of the planets which orbited it. This idea had never been widely accepted because it opposed the views of the church and to do so, at that time, could ruin a scientist's career.

At the age of 17, Galileo enrolled in the University of Pisa in Italy, where he studied the mathematics and philosophy of the ancient Greeks. In studying Aristotle, who had been considered the authority on science for over 1,500 years, Galileo was determined to update the approach.

Unlike Aristotle, Galileo would use experiments to prove his theories.

At the age of 25, Galileo began teaching mathematics at the University of Pisa. He made enemies almost from the start. It was no secret that he thought that the science taught at the university — teachings based on Aristotle — was a lot of nonsense. He set about trying to disprove those age-old beliefs.

One of the statements in Aristotle's science said that heavier objects fall to the ground faster than lighter objects. Galileo went to the top of the leaning tower of Pisa where he released two cannon balls of different weight at exactly the same moment. When the two cannon balls struck the ground at the same time, Galileo was proven right. His enemies, however, refused to admit their error and devoted themselves to making Galileo's life difficult. Just three years after his appointment at the university, Galileo was forced to resign from his position and retire to Florence.

At a new job at the University of Padua, although envied and hated by many, Galileo was building a reputation as a scientific genius. Word spread across Europe. When a bright, new object appeared in the heavens in 1604, many scientists tried to explain what it was. Some said it was a meteor. Galileo, in a presentation to a large audience, proved that the bright object was not a meteor but a fixed star outside our solar system. With demonstrations and a series of publications on motion, astronomy, sound, light and color, Galileo's distinction grew — but with it came a growing army of enemies.

In 1609, Galileo learned that an optical instrument, which we now call a telescope, had been invented in Holland. Galileo worked on the creation of his own telescope, and with it, he made a series of outstanding discoveries. The moon, he found, was not the crystal sphere it was believed to be, but a twin earth, with mountains and craters. The stars, he saw, were "a host of other stars which escaped the naked eye, so numerous as to pass belief." He also discovered the moons of Jupiter and the rings of Saturn. Galileo proved once and for all that the sun and the planets do not revolve around the earth. He now openly accepted the heliocentric theory of Copernicus.

His discoveries, published in a book entitled *Sidereus Nuncius - Messenger of the Stars* catapulted him to the height of his fame. In 1611, the church's astronomers confirmed the existence of the moons of Jupiter, and Galileo was welcomed and honored in Rome. He might have thought his troubles were over, but in fact, the battle was just beginning.

Using the power of the church against him, his enemies set about their wicked deed of destroying Galileo's career. They quoted from the *Holy Scripture, Joshua, Book X, Verse 13,* "And the sun stood still...in the midst of heaven" and *Ecclesiastes Book I verse 4, "...* the earth abideth forever. The sun also ariseth and the sun goeth down and hasteth to his place where he arose." These quotes were interpreted to mean that the sun moved and so, therefore, Galileo's heliocentric theory violated the holy word. Galileo was guilty of heresy!

Pope Paul V warned Galileo not to continue his teachings and this warning was followed by an order not to "hold, teach or defend" the heliocentric view. Galileo heeded this warning for the next 16 years though he quietly continued recording the observations made with his telescope. Then, in 1632, he published a "best selling" book titled, *Dialogue on the Two Chief Systems of the World, the Ptolemaic and Copernican.*

There was an outcry from the Vatican! How could such a scandalous book be published!

Galileo, now 70 and extremely ill, was summoned from his sickbed to face the Inquisition in Rome. Dressed in the white sheet of penitence, he was forced to kneel down and "with a sincere heart and unfeigned faith, obscure curse and detest his errors and heresies." It is said, however, that as he walked away he muttered defiantly, "Eppur si muove" - But it moves just the same!

Galileo was forbidden to write any more on astronomy and was to be imprisoned, but the prison was to be his own house. Here, for the next 10 years, he worked on his theories of dynamics and laid the foundation of this science.

During his imprisonment, Galileo's health worsened. In 1637, after publishing *Dialogue on the New Science,* he wrote, "I am totally and irreparably blind. These heavens, this earth, this universe which by wonderful observation I had enlarged a thousand times beyond the belief of past ages, are henceforth dwindled into the narrow space which I myself occupy."

A priest wrote of Galileo, "The noblest eye which nature ever made is darkened."

The heliocentric theory which Galileo had championed was to be proved mathematically correct by a scientist who was born in the year that Galileo died - 1642. The scientist, believed by many to be the greatest mathematical scientist of all time, was named Sir Isaac Newton. When, near the end of his life, Newton was asked why he was able to see so far across the frontiers of science, he responded, "I have stood on the shoulders of giants." One of the giants to whom Isaac Newton was referring, was Galileo Galilei.

CAPT'N EASY

Winning the Congressional Medal of Honor means that a U.S. soldier displayed "courage above and beyond the call of duty." But putting one's life on the line is not always enough. It often means using one's ingenuity.

On a cold February morning in 1951 on a windswept hill in South Korea, "Capt'n Easy" ordered the last bayonet charge in modern warfare. He would lead it into a murderous line of machine-gun fire.

Captain Lewis Millet was nicknamed "Capt'n Easy" by his men in U.S. Army Company E, mostly because he didn't believe in being easy at all. But when he asked his men to do something difficult, they knew that he would be doing it with them.

When Millet had first taken command of "Easy Company," the men had had very little training in the use of bayonets. "Capt'n Easy" soon changed all that. All the men were issued the murderous knives. Attached to the ends of their rifles, their guns were transformed into long swords or spears.

He drilled them hour after hour on how to use a bayonet in hand-to-hand combat. The men wondered why they bothered. After all, no one used bayonets anymore. What good were knives against rifles, machine guns and hand grenades?

But Millet wanted them to be prepared.

On that cold February morning, all their training would finally be put to use.

Millet and his men were pinned down by the enemy at the foot of a hill. The North Korean army was firmly entrenched in foxholes, using six machine guns and other weapons to fire on the Americans.

Millet called for a barrage of machine-gun fire. Under this protection, he called to his men, "Fix bayonets! Charge!"

Up the hill they stormed, with Millet braving the way. The North Koreans were firing down the hill while Millet's men were firing over their own heads up into the Korean lines. The noise, confusion and smoke from thousands of rounds of ammunition firing concealed their approach up the hillside.

Dodging Korean grenades, the Americans kept right on charging. Though Millet was wounded, he picked himself up, and although limping, he struggled on with the charge.

Suddenly, the North Korean soldiers looked up. Coming at them was a hellish nightmare! A platoon of yelling and screaming U.S. soldiers waving bayonets was the last thing they expected!

The mechanics of modern warfare were forgotten! Abandoning their machine-guns, the North Koreans either fled or rose to fight man to man. As though time had taken a giant leap backwards, the men struggled in hand-to-hand combat.

Though the North Koreans outnumbered the Americans, hundreds of them turned to run down the other side of the hill. They wanted no part of the crazed Americans and their bloody knives.

"Capt'n Easy" and his Easy Company took the hill. Of 97 dead Korean soldiers, 57 of them had died of bayonet wounds.

Four Americans died in the battle, and another four had been wounded. Though Captain Millet was one of these, he refused to let the medics work on him until his three men were treated.

Land Divers

A tall, lean diver stands poised on a narrow scaffold, 100 feet up from the ground. Vines called "woody lianas" wind around each foot tying him to the platform. In just moments he will dive. Leaping head first from the wooden tower, he will be suspended by the strong vines. If the attempt is successful, his head should just touch the ground. If the vines were cut too long, however, his neck will be broken on impact with the earth.

Below, dancers chant and sing. The diver, as though in a trance, gazes in concentration. Then, reaching into his belt he takes a sprig of leaves, waves them above the waiting crowd and tosses them earthward. The singing and dancing stop. The diver is about to prove his manhood.

Leaping from his platform of less than 16 inches wide, he dives to the speed of 45 miles per hour. At last, tension from the long flowing vines, slows the diver's fall. Just as his head touches the ground, the vines are pulled taut, recoiling the diver back from the ground, safely!

The chanting, singing and dancing resumes, followed by feasting and celebration. Although this ritual takes place yearly on the Pentacost Island of the Pacific, amazingly, not one death has yet occurred.

Flight 90's Anonymous Hero

"We're not going to make it!"

Those were the last words of pilot Larry
Wheaton. Seconds later, Air Florida Flight 90,
struggling to gain altitude in the middle of a
blizzard, crashed just after takeoff in
Washington, D.C. on January 14, 1982. The
doomed plane struck a bridge and plunged into
the icy Potomac River.

The plane, with 74 passengers and 5 crew, was heading for the 14th Street Bridge, which was packed with late-afternoon commuter traffic. Motorists didn't have a chance to react. The plane, with its nose up and tail down, struck the bridge with a thundering jolt. Parts of the plane sliced off the tops of cars and trucks. Four people were killed instantly. Crushed and mangled vehicles and bodies were strewn about the pavement. The bridge looked like a combat zone.

"It hit the bridge and just kept on going like a rock into the water. It was so loud I couldn't hear myself scream," was how Lloyd Creger described it.

He was driving by when the plane crashed. "The pilot," he added, "was trying like hell to get that jet up."

But too much ice on its wings had forced the plane down. There was nothing the pilot could have done to save it. Leaving a mass of destruction behind it on the bridge, the plane crashed through the ice of the Potomac River. In just moments it was gone! All that could be seen was its broken tail section, jabbing up out of the frigid water.

Clinging to the exposed tail of the plane, six people, still miraculously alive following the impact of their crash, were stranded. Five of them would be rescued and they would owe their lives to the sixth, a man whose name they'd never know.

The survivors and those who watched helplessly from the bridge would remember only that the hero was a balding man in his fifties. Without a thought for his own survival, it seemed, he helped the other five to safety. Those who witnessed the courageous deed were overwhelmed at his self-sacrifice.

When a rescue helicopter arrived and lowered a rope with a rescue ring attached to it, the balding man was the first to reach it. Instead of clinging to the rescue ring, he passed it on so another passenger could be hauled to safety.

Priscilla Tirado grabbed on to the rescue ring that would lift her to safety. Slowly, she began to rise but, trembling with fear, she lost her grip and plunged into the icy water with a scream!

A government clerk, Lenny Skutnik, who was driving by when the plane hit, saw the woman drop. Courageously, he jumped into the freezing water after her. Struggling with the weight of his heavy clothes, he reached her. Although Priscilla Tirado's state of panic made the return swim even more difficult, Skutnik managed to drag her to safety.

Meanwhile, the helicopter hovered over the remaining people trapped on the tail section. Again and again it lowered the rope with the rescue ring and each time the balding man passed it on to the other passengers. Although the plane's tail was rapidly sinking and the icy water crept higher and higher, the anonymous hero stood by, assisting each one until they were secured by the rescue ring. With the fifth passenger pulled to safety, the balding man clung to the tip of the plane's tail. Already he was immersed in the freezing water, but he clung there, silently awaiting the helicopter's final return.

At last, when the helicopter circled around to the site of the wreck, the tail section had disappeared beneath the ice. Gone with it was the hero.

He was one of the 74 passengers who lost their lives, but while most of them died strapped into their seats and trapped beneath the icy Potomac, this unknown man died helping others to live.

LANDING

Joe Lippo concentrated on the small plane flying low, right above his head. In a dangerous bid to save the pilot's life, he had to reach it — he had to pull that wheel loose!

As Joe Lippo stood up in an open car that was racing down the runway at 90 miles per hour, the driver of the car grasped Lippo's legs with one arm to keep him from flying out. Then Lippo strained upward toward the plane. The 26-year-old airplane mechanic said later, "I had some things on my mind, like the airplane dropping suddenly, or the back of the plane hitting me on the head!"

It was March 12, 1984, a pleasant day out at the St. Augustine, Florida, airport — until they learned about Scott Gordon.

Gordon, a young pilot, was preparing to land when one of the plane's three wheels wouldn't come down! If he tried to land with the wheel up, he would probably be killed!

It was airport manager Jim Moser who came up with the daring plan, and after studying it, Joe Lippo agreed to help.

Moser got a car with a sunroof and started driving along one of the runways. Gordon was directed to fly right above him. With both plane and car going at breakneck speed, Gordon lowered the plane until it was almost on top of the car.

That's when Lippo stood up and started yanking on the airplane's stuck wheel! "Joe grabbed the wheel," Moser said, "gave it a mighty tug and locked it in the down position." Scott Gordon landed safely.

As Moser put it: "It was pretty amazing."

Madeleine De Vercheres

Old friends of the family called her Mademoiselle Magdelon, a childhood name that stuck as she grew into adolescence. In little more than a week she would be widely known as Mademoiselle Mari-Madeleine de Vercheres, the woman who singlehandedly held battle with the Iroquois.

About fifteen miles from the settlement of Montreal was the home and estate of Madeleine's father. He was away on business for some days, and Madeleine's mother was staying in Montreal. It was October 22, 1692. Dead leaves crushed under her feet as she approached her family's fort. Suddenly, she stopped. Guns were firing!

"Fly, mademoiselle, fly! The Iroquois are upon us!" cried a servant.

Madeleine turned to see an army of Iroquois running toward her. Realizing she could not outrun them, she made a dash for the fort. It was her only chance.

Bullets whizzed by her ears as the ground blurred below! She was running faster than she'd ever run in her life! She was running with the speed of lightning and, yet, the distance to the fortress gates was never greater. In moments that seemed endless she uttered prayers under her breath until, finally, beneath her fingers, she felt the rough wood of the gates.

"To arms! To arms!" she cried, but no one answered her call. The fort's windows were dark and empty. As she ran toward the door she wondered if they were all dead. Had the Iroquois taken her two little brothers? Where were the soldiers?

People were crying, and husbands lay dead before her. Ushering the weeping wives inside, she bolted the door behind her. It was far too early, however, to breathe a sigh of relief.

Two soldiers were found lying low in the guard-house, cowering with fear. They at first jumped willingly to Madeleine's orders, glad to have some direction. But was this woman not crazy? they wondered. Did she really think they — a handful of people — could have a chance against a vast band of Iroquois? The answer was "yes."

"Let us fight to the death for our country and for our holy religion," she shouted. "Remember what our father has so often told you - that gentlemen are born but to shed their blood for the service of God and the king!"

With that, Madeleine's two little brothers each seized a musket and took up watch at the guard-house windows. The two soldiers, shamed into action, took up their posts. Madeleine ordered that the cannon be fired, and her small army kept up a steady attack on the enemy. One soldier, who had never fired a gun before,

learned fast how to aim. And Madeleine learned that her instinct for survival left no time for fear. Taking a musket herself, she took up position at a window. As her gaze took in the terror of their predicament, she spotted a canoe approaching on the river. It was her friend Pierre Fontaine!

What seemed for a moment to be good fortune turned before her eyes into a nightmare! If Pierre and his family were not warned, she realized, they would be taken by the Iroquois when they came ashore. She had to warn them.

She sneaked out to greet them and returned safely with the new recruits. Pierre Fontaine took a musket and joined in the fire. Below, the Indians fell, and then withdrew — but they weren't gone. Thinking the fort was well-manned, they decided to wait until nightfall for their attack. They would not have believed that they were being held off by seven people, two of them boys, and its leader, a girl of fourteen!

But Madeleine had no fear. ". . . to show you that I am not afraid, I undertake the fort for my share with an old man of eighty and a soldier who has never fired a gun." That night, never stopping even for a moment's rest, Madeleine kept watch, her eyes and ears picking up the slightest movement and noise.

The Iroquois were later to have said that, though they had planned to attack the fort that night, "the increasing vigilance of the guard" had deterred them.

Without rest or food, Madeleine and her small crew kept a strong defense. Although the Iroquois had retreated, she ordered the cannon to be fired every hour to alert any help that might come from Montreal.

At last, on the seventh evening of the raid, an army of forty men came to her rescue. Upon greeting the officer in command, Lt. De La Monnerie, she said, "Sir, you are welcome, I surrender my arms to you."

"Mademoiselle," he said, "they are in good hands."

"Better than you think," said Madeleine.

Lion Fight

Ndaka was a tracker, not a hunter. Through the African plains and jungles he moved stealthily, his only weapon a six-inch knife. He was there only to lead the hunters to their prey. When a lion, a leopard or other large game were found, the rifle-toting hunters would attack with a stream of bullets. But what happens when the animal attacks instead, as it did one day in August, 1961?

Ndaka watched as John Kingsley-Heath, a hunter, struggled with the ferocious jaws of a wounded lion. Flung about by the arm, Kingsley-Heath cringed in pain. The lion's claws tore his clothing and cut deep into his flesh.

"Get my gun!" he yelled in desperation. "Hit the thing! Shoot it!"

The other hunter, Bud Lindus, fired. Both he and the other tracker - who did have a gun - had fired their shot already but angered the lion even more! The other tracker fired again, but unsuccessfully. Now the guns were empty. Kingsley-Heath was being killed.

Ndaka had no choice. In moments, the tracker was upon the lion, stabbing it repeatedly in the ribs and throat. With his six-inch knife, he hacked away viciously at the wounded beast. He knew the others would have their guns reloaded soon. If he could get the lion away from Kingsley-Heath, and keep out of its reach himself, they'd be able to shoot it.

His plan worked! The lion was distracted. A shot fired and the lion went down.

Kingsley-Heath, with both arms broken, dragged himself to his feet. To push himself away from the dead beast, he jabbed his foot into its face. But the lion wasn't dead! In a last surge of revenge, it bit into Kingsley-Heath's shoe, crushing his foot and ankle!

Though Kingsley-Heath's arms and foot would heal, and the terror fade with time, one thing would always be with him. He would always have the deepest respect for Ndaka the tracker.

43

PT 109

A patrol torpedo boat is no bigger than many pleasure boats. The navy used these boats in the Second World War because they were small, fast and could easily be concealed while patrolling islands and coastal areas. Their most important function was to move in close to large enemy ships, release torpedoes and escape as quickly as possible.

John F. Kennedy was captain of such a patrol boat, numbered PT 109.

It was March, 1943. For a week, Lt. Kennedy's boat patrolled the waters known as Blackett Strait. In the still of the night, the little boat found its way directly in line with a huge Japanese destroyer.

The massive steel hull of the ship cut the water toward them at a great speed! One of the PT 109's crew fumbled with a 37-millimeter gun on deck, but realized that by the time the shell was loaded into the gun…it would be too late!

The commander of the Japanese destroyer Amagiri ordered his crew to ram the PT boat. As the bow of the Amagiri drove through the PT 109, a deafening crash filled the air. The PT boat was sliced in half! Lt. Kennedy, who had been standing on the forward half of the boat, was thrown from the wheel, striking a steel brace with his back. He recovered from the pain in time to see the PT's stern sink quickly under the weight of its engines.

Two of Kennedy's crew were killed instantly. Others were severely burned as they tried to swim from the flaming gasoline around the hull. Lt. Kennedy, though his back was badly injured, dived into

the dark waters to rescue his crewmen. Finally, he got the men aboard what remained of their boat and there they huddled...waiting.

All night, Lt. Kennedy wondered what they should do. In their present predicament, drifting aimlessly on the wreck of a boat, they were extremely vulnerable. They could not stay there, he decided. When the sun rose over the horizon of the Pacific, Lt. Kennedy told his men that if they didn't try to swim to one of the nearby islands, they would likely be captured by the enemy. They were a pitifully easy target.

He chose Plum Pudding Island, 3 1/2 miles through shark-infested waters, and hoped that the island was not inhabited by Japanese troops.

Although the plan seemed their only alternative, some of the men were too weak to make the journey. A few would not be able to swim at all, Kennedy realized, and so he found a large floating plank on which the injured men could ride.

Patrick McMahon, however, because of severe burns, had not even the strength to hold onto the plank. Lt. Kennedy fitted a vest onto him. Attaching a large strap to McMahon's vest, Kennedy took the other end of the strap in his teeth, dragging the man through the water behind him.

Kennedy was determined to make it. His jaws ached, his arms and legs were numb and at times he came close to losing consciousness.

Four hours later, Lt. Kennedy and McMahon drifted ashore, panting and exhausted on the sand. The others on the plank soon followed.

When the crew was finally rescued, Lt. Kennedy was promoted. He was awarded both the Navy and Marine Corps medals for his courageous act and the honor of the Purple Heart.

A Priest's Last Prayer

Prisoner Number 16670 huddled in a corner shivering. Two weeks earlier there had been 10 of them in Death Cell 11 - now there were only six. Although the Nazi guards had removed the bodies of the four others, the stench of death remained.

Number 16670 was the number the Nazis had given Maximilian Kolbe. To destroy his identity they'd taken his name, but they could not take his character. Inside Kolbe was something so strong that it could not be stolen, killed, or bought - this something was the strength to do what was right, what Kolbe knew was right. Because of this inner strength, Kolbe, a Polish Catholic priest, was now in the Death Cell.

The Nazis had invaded Poland in 1939. They arrested hundreds of thousands of people: some for being Jews, some for being gypsies, some for being priests.

Kolbe had been arrested in February of 1941 and declared "an enemy of the people." He was a Catholic priest and that "crime" would be dealt with severely.

After several months in a Warsaw prison, he was transferred to Auschwitz. Locked inside a cattle car with 304 other prisoners, he traveled to the dreaded concentration camp where in two years, between 1942 and 1944, four million people would be exterminated.

As they were marched inside the camp, they saw the sign over the gate: "Arbeit Macht Frei," which translates to: "Work Makes You Free." Then they saw the searchlights and the guards in the watchtowers with their machine guns. Surrounding the camp was an electric wire fence powerful enough to kill anyone who touched it. No one would escape.

Kolbe was taken to an area where his head was shaved. He was forced to take off all his clothes. Everyone took a shower together in a huge room. He was given a cap, wooden shoes and ill-fitting, tattered and dirty clothing. His prisoner number, 16670, was tattooed on his arm.

Then the work, torture and starvation began. Kolbe was put on a work detail in which he had to push wheelbarrows filled with gravel all day. The prisoners received a cup of tea or coffee in the morning, a meager portion of watery vegetable soup at lunch, and another cup of tea or coffee, a piece of bread and, if they were lucky, a piece of sausage for supper.

Although it was hardly enough for anyone to live on, Kolbe often gave his food to other prisoners he thought needed it more.

For two months, this was Kolbe's life. Then, one night, a prisoner escaped and the guards decided that those left behind would pay for it.

First, they took away the prisoners' food - it was poured down the drain before their eyes.

The next day they were forced to stand out in the hot sun. They were starving and exhausted as the intense heat beat down on them. Some of the prisoners fainted and one by one they were piled on top of each other in a heap.

Then the camp commander marched out to them with yet another punishment - ten men would die in place of the one who had escaped!

Slowly, the commander walked the long lines of prisoners and, with a flick of a finger, randomly picked one man, then another. An officer followed, writing down the number of each man chosen, and that prisoner stepped quietly to one side.

Not a sound was heard until the camp leader chose Francis Gajowniczek.

The man cried out, "No! I'll never see my wife and children again!"

The Nazis ignored him. Kolbe didn't. Stepping out of the line, the priest took off his cap and whispered to the commander.

"I am a Polish Catholic priest," Kolbe said. "I am old. I want to take his place, because he has a wife and children."

Gajowniczek, trembling with fear, stepped back into line and Kolbe took his place as a substitute victim.

Two weeks later, Kolbe and four others were still alive — barely — with just enough strength to sing and pray together. Their stomachs shrunken from starvation, they no longer felt the sharp pangs of hunger. And their hearts, without hope, accepted their end. Although their voices were weak and their songs made but a faint melody, even this show of spirit was too much for the Nazis. Besides, the cell was needed for other prisoners.

The camp "doctor" arrived to give each prisoner an injection -- of poison. When it was his turn to die, Prisoner number 16670 held his left arm out to receive the shot. He made no complaint - just a prayer. Perhaps his last words were for a peaceful world.